CRITTER FITTER™

With Bizzy Bee!

An Adventure in ... ment

CRITTER FITTER™

With Bizzy Bee! *An Adventure in Movement*

Authored by Dr. Jen Welter
Illustrated by Brooke Foley
A Jenny Football Production, Publisher

This book is dedicated to all the important critters in our lives that inspired this series to begin with: Carly, Danny, Chloe, Tyson.

Special Thanks to Amanda Matthews

Every day just like you,

bugs get up with bug things to do.

Bizzy is a bee who stays busy.

She loves to move and help make honey.

"From all of the critters and the way they move,

I got into my exercise groove.

Yes, I know, I can sting.

But, exercise is my favorite thing."

What a great day to be Bizzy the Bee!

There were flowers as far as Bizzy could see.

Bizzy was busy flying around,
she saw something on the ground.

Bizzy bee-lined, flying down.

She had to help, the kids faces had frowns.

Flowers were calling, but the kids looked so sad.

She couldn't leave, she would feel too bad.

The kids were scared.

"Bizzy Bee, please don't sting."

Bizzy smiled.

"*Talk to the wing, stinging is not my thing.*

I just flew over to check on you,

we have so many more fun things to do."

"*I fly all day through the air,
there are ideas everywhere.*

Every time I look at a critter,
I get an idea how to get fitter!"

"Bizzy you are teasing, you know that's not fair.

We don't have wings, we can't come fly up in the air."

After some thinking, Bizzy knew the right thing to do.

"If you can't go to the critters, the critters will come to you!"

The kids looked at Bizzy with a whole lot of fear.

"Bizzy, our parents won't let us have critters in here!"

Bizzy laughed and she got a big, big smile.

Bizzy laughed harder than she had in a while.

"You don't have to go where I go to see what I see.

I will teach you to get Critter Fitter like me!"

The first thing you do to be a Bizzy Bee,
is to warm up your wings, just like me.

If you are tight, you will not fly right,
and that is not a pretty sight!

Time to warmup, this warmup is honey-sweet.
Come on, critters, let's start with the feet.

Here's how this one goes,
rock from your heels up to your tippy toes.

For all my little Bizzy Bees,

One leg up at a time, hug your knees.

Next to the back, heels up please.

Next we move on to our wings, round in circles, make some rings.

Make sure you circle them forward and back,
then get ready for the DIZZY BIZZY attack!

Spin around five times, then you will sway...

Then take your stinger and swing it this way!

Three times forward and back,
side to side, then stop.

Last but not least, a round of applause for me and for you,

then we've got our Critter Fitter exercises to do.

Around the corner and up a tree.

A wise owl whooos, "Are you who'ing for me?"

We've ruffled her feathers,

so we ruffle together!

Then Owl whooo'd as her wings spread wide,

Displaying those feathers with owl pride.

"Let's get those wings all flappin',

When we move, good things will happen."

Flap your wings up high and down low,

Flap until, you can't flap no mo'.

We shake our tailfeathers, wings, and all critter things.

Up top we shake shake, until we can't anymore,

with a one, a two, a three and a four.

Now that you've shaken and your wings are flapped out,

Your next critter will come crawling about.

We were up flapping, now look down.
See the inchworm, inching around?

To inchworm around, bend over and put your hands down.
Inch your hands out, until you are out flat like the ground.

Keep your hands out, now inch your feet in.
Bring them together, then inchworm again.

As inchworms we love inching on the floor,

While on the ground we can do even more.

Time to roll-over, face up to the sky.

And we inch up, crunching high.

Once you have inched out, feeling fitter on the floor,

Another critter is ready to show you some more.

One hop, two hop, one... two... three...

Hidey Hop, just like this super shy bunny.

At first he tries hard to stay hidden away,

But once we make friends he will bunny hop all day.

Left hop, right hop, bunny hop drop!

Left hop, right hop, bunny hop drop!

There are lots of hops we can do.
Try it with one leg and try it with two!

Hop out, hop about, hop til you're through,

Let's get fitter with another critter for you.

Before Bizzy let another critter come to the room,

With a bark and a wag, the dog bounded in too soon.

Pets are critters who need exercise too.

This time the kids knew just what to do.

Bizzy taught them to get on all fours, showed them to chase their tail.

Then they guessed, "Now we go jump up on who's delivering the mail!"

Bizzy smiled. The kids were acting like critters and having fun.

They would sleep well after all the exercises they'd done.

The kids showed Bizzy all the things they thought a dog would do.

Then when they were wagged out, and barked out too,

Bizzy had one more thing to lead them through.

From your tummy, push up and rock back please,
Now walk your hands to your knees.

One knee out, support yourself and come up,
Now a deep breath as you bring those arms up.

Exhale and relax your arms down to your sides,
All that hard work should fill you with pride.

Another few deep breaths to finish the day,
A round of applause, hip hip hooray!

The kids heard their names called, and that was their cue.

After all, Bizzy still had her own work to do.

The kids were happy, no more frowns,

and Bizzy was happy because she flew down.

The kids thanked Bizzy for the fun day.

They asked her to promise that she wouldn't stay away.

Bizzy said,

"Oh kids, it was fun for me too,

and I have endless Critter Fitter

workouts for you!"

Made in the USA
San Bernardino, CA
26 June 2020